Praise for *To Shatter Glass*

"In this new collection of poems, rising as they do out of past turmoil and brokenness, Sister Sharon Hunter's meditations speak in redemptive ways, inviting us into the old wounds and scars and presenting to God, and to us as readers, fresh understandings of what it takes to heal."

—**Luci Shaw**, author, *The Generosity* and *Eye of the Beholder*, Writer in Residence, Regent College

"Sister Sharon's poetry leads her reader seamlessly through several chapters of life's most fearsome and heart-wrenching struggles to a place of redemption. The imagery that makes her poetry a visual experience keeps the reader hungry for the next scene, allowing just long enough to share her angst, while in the background a cadence pushes forward, promising the hope of redemption. The fact is, she may just be the most honest poet I have ever encountered."

—**Rev. Dr. Bradford D. Lussier,** pastoral counselor, author of *How Does He Love Me? A Collection of Love Sonnets*

"In words of courage, conviction, and terrible beauty, Sister Sharon Hunter dispels the myth of escaping life in the real world for the shelter of the cloister. She confronts the lingering demons of the past—a legacy of family alcoholism, abuse, violence, and depression—holding them up to the light of her daily encounters with the mysterious, often incomprehensible, love of God. By reading these poems, we are privileged to join her on the path to hope and healing."

—**Sister Helen Prejean,** author of *Dead Man Walking* and *River of Fire: My Spiritual Journey*

"Sister Sharon Hunter never forces us to swallow the 'wool pulled so far over our own eyes it's in our mouths,' yet she enables us to see the pain and hear the shattered glass that is our collective experience of loss. Her words respect this truth, but also give grace and hope to our individual hearts as we make pilgrimage together. Her courage expressed toward triumph through tears inspires us to keep going, believing in the goodness of God."

—**Margaret Philbrick,** Redbud Writers Guild, Contributing Editor of *Everbloom: Stories of Living Deeply Rooted and Transformed Lives*

"Unabashed is the first word that comes to mind to describe this debut poetry collection. Courageous is the second. With unflinching candor Hunter here lays bare the despair, destruction and shattering loss she experienced growing up in an alcoholic home. But this recounting is far more than a chronicle of personal loss and pain. Rather it is the beginning of a pilgrimage of hope and restoration to which she bids readers join her, poem by poem, and step by step."

—Margaret B. Ingraham, author of *Exploring This Terrain*

"There's not an ounce of affectation or pretentiousness in these poems. They have a 'Mary Oliver' directness. One poem, 'The Listener,' thanks the person who hears a broken heart and finds the unshed tears in our nervous laughter. These poems do exactly that, they hear your broken heart and help you name your unshed tears. Poems give clear expression to unclear feelings. These poems do that. Wonderfully."

—Ronald Rolheiser, OMI, author of *Bruised and Wounded*, *The Fire Within*, and *Domestic Monastery*

"*To Shatter Glass* not only breaks literal doors, but also trauma-related silences. A memoir in verse, *To Shatter Glass* honors the holy mystery of its subject matter by avoiding superfluous details. Instead, Sister Sharon offers 'life's fragments,.../ like ice floes from a half-frozen river.' One of these fragments is the miracle that 'Any day now, a bird will lift its tiny head and sing.' Sister Sharon Hunter is that bird, and her song enriches all who hear it."

—Melanie Weldon-Soiset, poet, former pastor, and #ChurchToo spiritual abuse survivor

TO SHATTER GLASS

Poems

Sister Sharon Hunter, CJ

Christmas 2021
To Macy,
Wishing you peace like a
river, the joy of a song.

Love and fond
memories,
Sr. Sharon

IRON
PEN

Brewster, Massachusetts

2021 First Printing

To Shatter Glass: Poems

Copyright © 2021 by The Community of Jesus, Inc.

ISBN 978-1-64060-714-9

The Iron Pen name and logo are trademarks of Paraclete Press.

Library of Congress Cataloging-in-Publication Data
Names: Hunter, Sharon, 1947- author.
Title: To shatter glass : poems / Sister Sharon Hunter, CJ.
Description: Brewster, Massachusetts : Paraclete Press, [2021] | Summary:
  "Poems from a heart searching for healing and love; searching for God"–
  Provided by publisher.
Identifiers: LCCN 2021013375 (print) | LCCN 2021013376 (ebook) | ISBN
  9781640607149 (trade paperback) | ISBN 9781640607156 (epub) | ISBN
  9781640607163 (pdf)
Subjects: LCSH: Autobiographical poetry, American. | Christian poetry,
  American. | BISAC: POETRY / Women Authors | RELIGION / Christian Living
  / Personal Memoirs | LCGFT: Poetry.
Classification: LCC PS3608.U594964 T6 2021 (print) | LCC PS3608.U594964
  (ebook) | DDC 811/.6--dc23
LC record available at https://lccn.loc.gov/2021013375
LC ebook record available at https://lccn.loc.gov/2021013376

10 9 8 7 6 5 4 3 2 1

Published by Paraclete Press
Brewster, Massachusetts
www.paracletepress.com

Manufactured by Regent Publishing Services Ltd., Hong Kong
Printed June 2021 in Shenzhen, Guangdong, China

In love and gratitude for Mother Betty Pugsley,
Prioress of the Community of Jesus, 1989–2021.
Her love of the arts and pursuit of excellence in service
to God unlocked the door of my heart. I was set free
to search for beauty in life's complicated tapestry.

Contents

I

And So, I Begin

And so, I begin to make sense of the years through pen on paper. Words emerge and trace a journey, moving forward and backward, lingering like the pen, on occasion, at a resting place.

Travel with me.

Travel to places dark, painful, and without resolution. Each word is written with specific intention, searching out the secrets of hearts sometimes broken, but held together, unsevered. Life is a journey, part sunshine, part storm . . . and I'm honestly not sure which I prefer.

A Poet You Say?

I ponder this possibility:
poetry is a lazy man's memoir.
I say what I think, feel, or fear
with brevity of sentence,
without page upon page.
Many things can be said
with one word, if I give it thought.
"Help," being one of them,
"Forgive," another.

Am I unfair to poets?
In their flowery language,
Are they hesitant to expand
grimmer and greater things of life?
Perhaps, instead, their shorthand is selfless,
allowing the reader to interpret
and experience
according to *their* need.

Jigsaw Puzzle

Three years before completion, I began.
It's no easy task
to piece together life's fragments,
scattered across the table
like ice floes from a half-frozen river.
Swiftly moving,
difficult to capture,
broken
into lesser chunks
upon contact.

I recovered remnants
of an alcohol-driven childhood,
led by adults
more damaged than their offspring.
Cars weaved from lane to lane,
as if searching for sobriety.
Terrified kids huddled like unwashed
laundry on the rear seat floor.

Trampled feelings, devoid of pride,
don't say the proper things:
that I'm loved,
safe and worthy.
Snap.
A piece fits perfectly.
Marriage portrait.
A young bride and groom.

An unhappy couple,
worried a mistake just happened.
It did.

A stretch of time, marking time.
Waiting for the inevitable end
of wedded incivility.
Shouting,
cursing,
degradation,
pulls at the hem of my mind,
threatening to unravel a tentative hold on reality.
I'm submitted to locked doors
and mind-dulling drugs
that escort me to deeper isolation.
Dignity and respect
obliterated by well-earned abuse.

Escape imminent and necessary.
On to a new life with the old
still attached like a kudzu vine,
choking out the promise
of a fresh start.
I long for reprieve
from puzzle pieces
void of commonality.

II

Orphanos

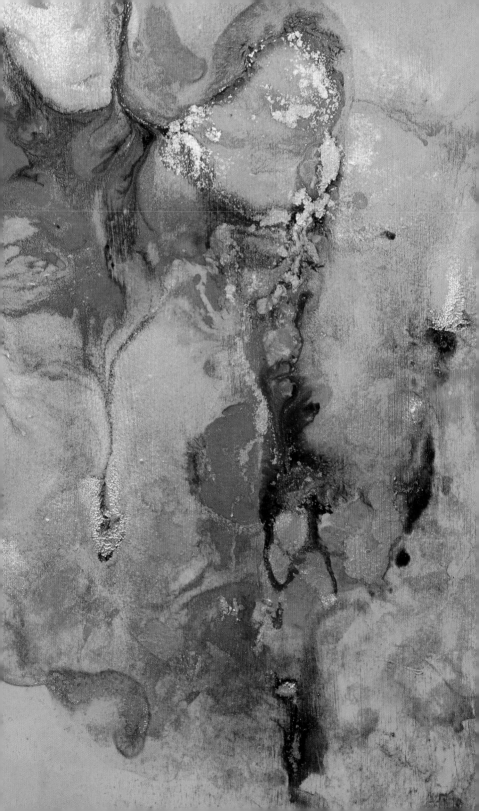

The Pretender

I wear a wounded heart on tattered sleeve,
and play pretend with all I can deceive.
I wear a wounded heart on tattered sleeve,
and sell my goods to those who will believe.
I make amends where none are needed.
I take the blame, for I've conceded,
life that's lived when scarcely shaded
leaves the ancient scars unaided.

When I was Three

The light went out when I was three
and I, the child, ceased to be
a child – yet child still, I played a game,
convincing myself that I was the same.

My soul was free though justly worn,
when tumbling in the thistle-thorns.
I watched the sky from upside down,
well hid where I could not be found.

Within myself, within a shell,
as secret as the deepest well,
quiet dreams of *should have been*
danced without and cried within.

Radical Change

I pursue his affection,
despite imperfection,
both my own and his.

A product of anxiety,
I survive because I can.

My Dad teaches us it doesn't
cost a penny to be kind.
He dispenses quarters, kites,
candy bars, and sound advice.
All things he lacks.

Sometimes he trips
on his personal demons,
disappearing into a drink-infested
relationship of distant formality
that leaves no space for children.

He staggers in disgrace, no longer
an object of secure admiration.
Insults slur my direction
once I pose a simple question.
A simple question, really.
Why?

By birth and name, I belong to him,
And I must, or I belong to no one.
I conform to his best and worst.
Today I am clothed in Sunday.
I stand dressed in the mismatched
remnants of a Saturday night binge.

The Neglected

We walk a maze of murdered dreams,
brimming with bankrupt imaginations
of children ignored.
We search for someone to hear us,
to interpret a version of events we've come to believe
with feverish insistence.

Unresolved incidents tease and circle
like sand gnats at the beach,
loathsome,
determined to keep their territory.
It's not enough, this confusion we
appropriate.

We won't survive
a lifetime of it, everyone dancing
their tune of murky unreality.
The composition lacks
veracity and nobility.
Wool pulled so far over our eyes
it's in our mouths
and we're forced to swallow it.

The Listener

There are those who listen, found infrequently
among an abundance of talkers, eager to offer
opinions and advice, well-intended but remiss.
They drown me in reckless counsel, stolen
from half-truths "safe enough" to share.
I fool most people, most of the time,
but not The Listener.

He hears a broken heart, finds
unshed tears within my nervous laughter.
Waiting with patient intent, he offers space
and significance to painful words encased in pride,
like long-dead bugs in amber.
Hands reach out, unconstrained, to catch the
important utterance of the voiceless invisible.
The Listener restores earth's obliquity;
I tilt in a safe direction,
no longer left to tumble
into fabricated chaos
I so deftly made my own.

Of This I'm Certain

My favorite color is deep blue.
The question asked, worthy to pursue.
Though it seems unessential,
for all I love or value, it's the glue.
Eternal. Indispensable blue.

On a sunny day near a wind-swept sea,
a child's eyes look out at me, as if to ask
are you empty?
Have you any love to spare?
For shells can walk and talk and smile,
and all the while,
their minds are
elsewhere . . .

What to say,
when to say it,
how to please and not betray,
to cover shadows of the day.
That's why it matters when I knew,
my favorite color was deep blue.

III

Hardly an Oyster

A Better Choice

I am the glass half-empty,
the tarnish on the silver lining,
nobody's sunshine on a cloudy day.
I'm adept at finding what's missing or could go
    wrong.
Worry is my addiction, crippling and unfruitful.
When born, on a cold October morning,
I hit the open air thinking, "Uh oh."
There were valid reasons, but there always were.

Jesus came to us fragile, helpless,
and surrounded by dangerous circumstances.
What if He
had arrived
worried?

Every Other Sunday

My uncle was seduced by the charm
of a ramshackle farm,
set well back from the highway.
It sported a murky frog pond,
decaying barn with three cows,
a pinto pony, a John Deere tractor
and a hay wagon.
A freshwater spring ran cold and free
through the house itself.
It was magic to reach down and fill a cup
before the molecules flowed beyond reach,
escaping tyrannical lips
of thirsty children.

Gray house inside and out,
upstairs and down.
Every trace of color
beneath the fine dust of unhappiness.
Gloom hovered like a bird of prey.
Problems postponed with quick hellos,
and screen doors slammed on our way out.
Fields to cross, fences to jump,
trees to climb, sweet-smelling fresh air.
We'd saddle up ancient Pancho
and slow-walk around the pasture.
When parents were out of sight,
we'd take a quick taste of salt lick.

The jewel of the tired estate
was my cousin Becky.

Born with fetal hydrocephalus
before the invention of the shunt,
her future fell into orbit
around faulty brain function.
Becky accepted suffering
like a bouquet of forest violets
from God himself.

She rested in a hand-carved bed,
its high-built sides encapsulating her.
She smiled at her healthy, young cousins,
and spoke reassuring words.
We pondered the wonder of her all.
Somehow, we knew we'd caught ourselves
a delicate,
beautiful
angel.

Little Children of Adult Alcoholics

We are the quiet ones,
the mediocre children
who hold excellence
purposefully within.
Too afraid to succeed,
too numb to utter the word "help."
We coax our minds to accept havoc.

We are the master pretenders.
Santa IS coming.
Just as soon as Mother remembers
where she hid the gifts.
Another glass of scotch.
It'll come to her.
. . .
Even she can't forget Christmas.

We are the sad-eyed ones,
forgetting to laugh at the joke.
Abandoned by our peers,
would-be friends who decide,
rightfully so,
we're not much fun after all.

We build bridges of snow
across teardrop rivers,
to fend off time as we play.
When the sun slides into night,
we join our parents

in their rendition
of what kids need.

Welcome to the Kennedys,
the Smiths and the Joneses.
You'll never know us.
We guard family secrets and absorb
everyday absurdities like cotton swabs
mopping up a mud puddle.

'Tis The Season

One small favor.
Will you pass me by this year?
It's a complicated season, Christmas.
Presents?
Sometimes they're there
and sometimes they're not.
Decorations?
Always in place.
Dishes of chocolates
and mixed-nuts aplenty.
But it's the mixed *drinks* that steal
the sparkle from the tree
and the joy from soft-sung carols.

I prefer the routine
of everyday sameness.
It's easier that way,
expectation kept from the door
like the Big Bad Wolf it is.
But then . . .
But then we'd forego the manger!
We'd miss Baby Jesus,
surrounded by friendly cows
and sheep like on the farm.

Next door we cry, my sisters and I,
confused by the choices
others make for us.
We long for Christmas

filled with love,
absent nonsensical conflict.

Mid-December,
we create a kind of sign language.
Our fingers flash.
Warning! Booze Alert.
Eight bottles of Johnny Walker.
Left side kitchen cupboard. Fear.
No longer *if* but *when* insanity rules.
When it hits the house, game over.
Baby Jesus will be ignored,
like the other children,
as if back in the attic, collecting dust.
We'll stuff ourselves with chocolates,
and breathe a sigh of relief
when the last bottle dies of emptiness.

As Strong as Fragile

Do not fear the fragile
for they will not break.
They bend and twist
then straighten,
to begin to bend once more.

When's My Turn?

My Aunt Meg was city born and bred,
dropped in the middle
of a sparsely populated countryside,
expected to raise a mansion
from a decaying farmhouse
that likely saw no better days.
She rebelled against disarray
in the best way she knew how.

Her husband, however, found nirvana,
a place to play at farming
while simultaneously
hiding his love of "the drink" from the world.
He was respected,
awarded nominal positions of political import
while my Aunt honed the fine art
of passive revenge.
People are funny.
            Or are they?

To Shatter Glass

I had a thought to shatter glass.
I joined the line, my placement last.
As older children ran ahead,
I lingered with my plan instead.

At age nine, or maybe eight,
I eyed the door to contemplate
a clean attack, a victory lap.
I set the stage, and laid the trap.

Two steps back,
time to go
head-long plunge,
a piercing blow.
Hands and knees on shattered rain,
my head slipped through the broken pane.

Around my neck, a jagged crown,
I didn't move or make a sound.
If I wished an end to life,
the glass was sharper than a knife.

I knew no fear,
felt no remorse
enjoyed the power,
and the force.
"It was the wind," I calmly lied,
then let myself be led inside.

Fame Overwhelms Me

My sixth-grade teacher, Mrs. Brooke,
had topsy-turvy day on Fridays.
We wore mismatched clothes,
feasted on sugary snacks,
and had elongated recess.
She was the most wonderful teacher
a chubby student with teeth at all angles
could imagine.
She prepared us for THE NEXT STEP,
the local junior-senior high school,
age range twelve to eighteen.
Twenty if you count the Emery boys,
who learned patience through fishing
and applied it to graduating.

One day, we learned to vote by selecting
the most popular girl and boy in class.
I felt faint, I'd wanted so badly to win.
Let's be real, I told myself.
"They don't even know my name."
Classmate rejection can be a painful lesson.
But not this time.
This time, I was voted Most Popular Girl.
Not only couldn't I believe it,
I found a way to make it insulting.
"No one's jealous of an introverted fat girl," I reasoned.
"Especially one sporting teeth
designed for early-onset braces."
I discovered fame isn't that special if you keep it quiet.
And so I did.

Weighing Priorities

I asked my mother to make a dress,
to sew it with her own hands.
She made quilts
often sewing until her hands were so tight
she could barely clench her fist . . .
I was convinced she had the skill.
I'd seen her conquer many things
"beyond her scope."
She once repaired the mixer
and left two extra parts!
Drive a pick-up truck?
One time, I went along to learn
through squawks and flying feathers
why chickens cross the road:
to get as far away from my mother as possible.

"Please Mom," I begged. "You can do it!"
She maintained she was a novice,
had no idea about patterns and such.
I insisted, pleaded,
my imagination conjured a dress
of soft gray wool,
pink sweater draped casually
over my shoulders, a la Doris Day.
Maybe a strand of fake pearls
or "pop beads" as we called them then.
And so she worked. And swore.
And worked some more.
I can still see her,

cigarette dangling from her bottom lip
zipping along on her portable Singer.

The day came for the final try on.
I was excited, elated, confident,
as I slipped the dress over my head.
It battled valiantly, but so did I.
At last, I stood in my gray dress,
pink sweater now irrelevant.
One shoulder higher than the other,
left side sewn tighter than the right.
Seams that were supposed to meet
avoided one another,
prizefighters before the first punch.
It was situation impossible,
because my mother looked so pleased.
But Teenage Rat that I was, I ignored her
well-earned pride of accomplishment.

I had a choice to make.
Hide her creation in shame,
or see the love sans imperfection,
risking the savage stares of popular divas
proclaiming all the while,
"Yes, my mother is a clothing designer.
Self-taught.
Lovely, isn't it?"
I chose the lesser road,
tucking my mother's love
in the back of my closet,
never to be worn.
And my heart grew all the smaller for the deed.

IV

Threads of Depression

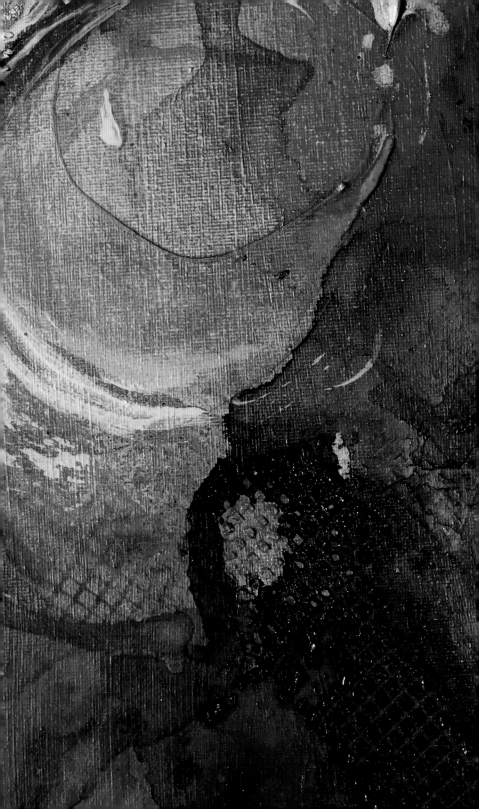

Home Remedy

I wake at three in the morning
obsessed with fly paper.
I wonder if it's still around.
In its heyday,
it resembled yellow corkscrew curls
like those worn by Shirley Temple.
The fly-curls dangled from the ceiling,
often over the table of all places,
sirens enticing common household flies
into a sticky death by starvation.
Nothing bolsters the appetite
like a collection of dying flies.

Depression is like fly paper;
it lures you to self-annihilation
through false advertising.
Stop on by, there's one place left
side-by-side with hundreds just like you,
wings outstretched, waiting.
It's safe up here,
away from the swatters
and the spray cans.
Hang out for a bit of isolation
and then discover that you're stuck
and going back,
if possible at all,
is extremely laborious.

Et Invisibilium

"Invisible" is my middle name.
I prefer it to all my others.
It better defines my persona
than Susan, Jennifer, or Alice,
all too common for someone
who desires not be known.
Think of all the juicy impossibilities.
"Here comes Invisible,"
"there goes Invisible,"
or my favorite,
"have you seen Invisible?"
But whatever my name,
they won't let me rest
until I find me.

Give It Back

Give me back what I had.
It wasn't much, I grant you,
but definitely more
than this dark,
unfamiliar haze.
Please change your mind.
I won't change mine.
I want *it* back.
Every
useless
bit of it.

Voice of the Inner Critic

Here is your nothing life.
Notice the zero on top.
It pairs quite nicely
with the zero on the bottom.

I don't presume to know
where the bottom is,
but if you've reached it,
I have no recourse for you.
No "better luck next time."
It's over, you're over,
and I must admit, I feel relief.
It's been boring,
boring as hell,
watching you atrophy.

I brought you a T-shirt.
It fits you perfectly.
See? It proclaims nothing.
Not even the word *Boston*,
where you've lived forty years.
No clubs, or hobbies or baseball teams.
Blank it is. And blank it remains
until death do us part.

Oh, Does It Hurt?

My eyes are swollen.
I'm allergic to medication prescribed
to make me "normal." His words.
My eyes are no longer occidental.
Instead, I resemble my Chinese friend,
who's thrilled I look like her. Her words.
She sees in me what I cannot,
and tells me things I wish were true.
Red patches slip down my cheeks,
like speckled burns from boiling water.

Another friend studies the damage.
"Oh, does it hurt?" she asks,
as if unable to imagine that it would.
Can I scream now?
I've always wanted to try it
but lack of practice keeps it subdued.
It simply bounces off the woodwork,
tumbles through the air, and dissipates,
inert mist unnoticed by those around it.
But let's go back to the question.
Does it hurt?
Mostly when I cry.

Litany of Know

I don't know.
I say it over
and over again.
Authorities on myself ask,
"What don't you know, silly?"
I have no answer.
"Where does it come from?"
I don't know.
"How could you not know?"
Unfortunately, I don't know that either.

Worthless Thief

A worthless thief lies curled within
the darkest corners of my heart.
He rears his hounds here,
feeds them, stokes them, uses them
to justify his intrusion in the syntax of my life.
The beasts
are smallness,
weakness,
silence,
invisibility.
Worthless thief, deceitful liar,
I know your name: Ego.
Un-fist the object in your hand!
That love was purchased
through suffering,
it has earned its right to be here.

Do as I Say

Tears will come and tears will sow.
They leave behind a field to grow.
Grain to feed a lifetime of regret,
a list of failures one cannot forget.

Move, you fool, life is short.
Move on and live, do not abort
this single chance of finding peace,
a way at last to find release.

Do I cry for you, or me?
Perhaps both.
Tears are free.
Is it the hunter or the prey
most in need of love today?

Forgive yourself,
you must forgive!
It's only then a man can live.
Love the answer.
Love the key.
Love that gives to you,
NOT me.

V

A Complicated Grief

Call Me

Let me chance to kindly offer
fewer words, absent coffers.
Lengthy phrase of consolation
will not soften desolation.
Explanations tend to differ,
well-placed words are simply swifter,
sharper than a surgeon's knife.
Brief description: end to life.
Let the telling do its best.
Let the matter come to rest.
She's gone.
She died on Sunday last.
The girl we love has cruelly passed.

The News Is Now Your Life

You hear it daily on the news.
Murder in the first degree
or perhaps the second.
Third or fourth,
what does it matter?
One murder. Multiple victims.
One dies, one lives, all suffer.
Murder is neither justifiable
nor rectifiable.
No further act fulfills the rage
of those left behind.

Here. Take the phone.
I cannot listen to lies
and irreversible truths.
I close my eyes,
swing shut my heart,
and stubbornly remain aloof
to this heinous crime.

The Visitor

When Evil comes calling,
don't let him in.
The face is familiar,
but the heart, twisted sin.

Oh, run to the neighbors,
run for your life!
He's hiding a stun gun,
a rope and a knife.

Death to a mother,
death by a son.
Death to a daughter.
Not one of whom won.

Please Ignore the Elephant

More tea? Another biscuit?
Try the chocolate.
Soooo delicious.
Lovely day, such weather!
I saw daffodils near the pond.
They're poisonous, did you know?
And tulips, just a few.
I like that color on you. Peach, is it?
And you brought chicken casserole.
Really? So thoughtful.
We'll serve it for supper tonight,
that is, if Helen stops by.
Not much for food these days.
Sometimes I feel I'll never eat again.

Broken Dreams

An unexpected reason to redeem,
scattered pieces of a broken dream.
Swatting voices, phantom foes,
we dance as flies on rotting rose.

Inward drama, outward action.
Unrest, deception, haunted faction.
Laughter stilted and pretended,
starting normal, normal ended.

Crying eyes that move to drying,
need more sense in senseless dying.
Hearts so wounded may not mend,
bound by chains that will not bend.

Wooden Man on Wooden Porch

You watched
the last dance
of light
in frightened eyes.
You heard the broken sigh,
ignored the final tear.

Vengeance pre-planned,
payback for insane acts,
innocent in thought,
horrible in function.
Judged guilty.
Maximum sentence.
Plotted by a wooden man
on a wooden porch,
who left a trail of blood
for others' grief to follow.

I'm not there,
but I imagine
the last dance of light
in forgiving eyes.
I hear the acceptant sigh,
catch the final tear.

Let justice, a cool cloth
cradled in God's hands,
come to a wooden man
on a wooden porch.

"Justice," because love
requires mercy
that trudges not
from my unforgiving heart.

Life after a Death

You have no idea how difficult it is
to relive the same devastating circle,
in the midst of depravity,
and not be identified
by its savage ugliness.

Shock sends me back
to the four walls of make-shift hell:
emotional instability, drunkenness,
violent confusion, dangerous action.

The way I live,
one plus one
will never equal two,
and I'm denied the right
to build a life spit-shined by unreality.

Left to Live

I do a comb-over
to hide the baldness of my soul.
I slap on a smile
to cover every avenue of sadness.
I tell a story.
Crack a joke.
I'm a child again,
covering the nothingness
I don't want you to see.

Papers in the Wind

We place our hope in passing time,
then test the measure of our mind.
Like papers rustling in the wind,
we contemplate another's sin.
Today forgive, tomorrow hate.
Shed our tears, await his fate.
Condolence holds no consolation,
only love bleeds inspiration.
Through turns, and jolts, we settle in,
papers nesting in the wind.

The Things I Called Her

My niece was tiny,
five pounds even.
I held her and she cried,
until we learned to trust.
I called her Sweet Girl.

She always loved horses.
First plastic, then real.
She'd take the reins
and I'd take the back,
more scared than thrilled.

She added imaginary pounds
and slimmed to nothing.
Beautiful, but flimsy.
Lovely, but unreachable.
I called her Sweet Shadow.

Voices captured her attention,
whispers of fear, chaos, danger,
silent to everyone but her.
She bled without bleeding,
cried without tears.

I called her Sweet Martyr.
In the end, the voices,
those crazy voices, spoke true.
Danger knocked
and she opened the door.

Too Late for Sorry

How sad a parting.
Can you forgive me?
Can I forgive me?
I turned deaf heart
to your tired voice,
and its small expectations.
You reached out
beyond your sickness
to touch solid ground.
But I said "no"
to another's illness,
and in doing so,
abandoned
fictitious voices
to silence.

She'd a brain that viewed the world
in psychedelic disorder.
Explosive mood changes drenched me
in breathtaking beauty
and unfathomable ugliness.
I was afraid of you,
a truth I'll regret
till I learn to forgive.

If Only

Unspoken words.
Unexpressed affection.
Shackled gifts so tiny
they'd fit in the palm of your hand.
They've power to change the world,
yet you toss the seeds in restless wind.

Choose Love

Ladybug, ladybug
fly back to me.
Your wings have touched
mountains and salty blue sea.

Oh, sing of adventure,
sing like a dove!
Sing how the darkness
is conquered by love.

Ladybug,
you won't fly back to me,
for your wings have brushed starlight.
Your spirit is free.

VI

Judas in Waiting

A Fence a Million Miles Away

Just north of here, along a fence
grapes grow beautiful and dense.
I eyed upon up-close inspection
symmetry that neared perfection.
Touched was I when I discovered,
each one nestled on the other.

I witnessed color transformation,
when I chanced by that location.
Each time I've eyed them furtively,
they've coexisted perfectly,
and in their doing,
beauty strong,
they all are one,
they all belong.

We are selfish as we journey,
always wanting, in a hurry.
Your quiet suffering doesn't grieve us,
we'd rather ask for you to leave us.
We trample where we ought to tend,
neglect, betray, instead of mend.

We are Judas. We are waiting.
We are stealing, we are taking,
not just gold, but lives worth living.
We'll ignore the love you're giving.
Our right to greed will not deny,
ours to have and yours to die.

Game of Spiders

Mr. and Mrs. Spider went up the waterspout.
They play a unique spider game.
I see what they're about.
They weave a web,
select a foe,
and lure her to their den,
declaring love and fellow-need,
then throw her out again.

"I'm for you, and you're for me
the others will not make it.
They are the pawns.
We set the rules,
and we're the ones that fake it.
So laugh with glee,
my darling spouse,
we've trapped us yet another.
We play a game of Mom and Pop
but we prefer each other."

I envy her that got away,
a product of your malice.
For all along she was the prey
the two of you so callous.
You waited but a bit too long
to pounce and claim your glory.
But on it goes and will so go,
this evil-minded story.

Love that hates and hateful love
doesn't bless or flourish.
Instead, it seeks to feed upon,
destroy and then self-nourish.

Shell Game

Who will buy what I sell?
It's hidden here beneath this shell.
Or this one, or is it that one there?
I've forgotten which or where.
Step right up. Have a try!
Hidden folds of dark deception
dull the sharpness of perception.
Come and wave your luck goodbye,
age and gender no exception.

Perhaps

The world was void.
Darkness covered the earth
before God said, "Let there be light."
Alone and afraid, we run from darkness.
Perhaps we should embrace it.
Perhaps in darkness, God's mystery is revealed.
Perhaps.

For hidden within its shapeless symmetry
is a pinpoint of light that woos and beckons.
Interior light
expanded through suffering,
unseen before its time.
It twirls like a ballerina, full of grace.
It etches a landscape, revealing the presence
of goodness, that never left.
We are a fresh canvas awaiting its artist,
a night sky awaiting its moon and stars.

When Those You Love

Not one small mind can comprehend
heartless and complete rejection.
Those you love and thought loved you
destroy your heart, obscure perception.

Greedy eyes forget the past,
the hours spent in their protection.
Possession – money is the goal.
They want it all, with no exception.

And so you sit and wonder why
they cast aside your trite affection,
call your mind an empty void
and hold clear thought in vast abstention.

When what is real cannot be fathomed,
fake a story you can mention.
Fake that all is what should be,
and live your life with this pretension.

Is It Possible

that this place, so devoid of the beauty I want for you, is
     perfect?
Here, minds can be collective, muddled, or missing altogether.
There is no Scorekeeper.
Don't despair, for you are loved, and this resting space,
an ungainly compilation of worn sheets, clumsy towels
and unrecognizable food
is somehow enough.
It requires little from you, but gives you time, reason,
     and freedom
from having to be present to protect the rest of us.
You deserve carefree simplicity, a polished stone,
resting in the worn and tired box of yesterday.
Don't fret, dear sister.
Don't worry that your hair isn't coiffed, your make-up perfect,
or that the same questions are asked and answers given.
I'll answer forever if it makes you feel secure.
Your soul is brave and your joy well-earned.
Thank you for everything.

Where Rot Cannot Reach

I understand.
I relate.
You offer kinship.
I accept.
We're not perfect,
either one,
but we've grown together
in our imperfectness.
On this stalk
are two wilted roses.
Both require the same sun,
the same water and steady hand
to thrive.

The Gaps Between

When I was but an infant child,
toothless, hairless, without guile,
my sister rocked me off to sleep,
singing songs of wooly sheep.

Mother had been busy then
with four young children left to tend
and another on the way.
"Will be the last," she'd often say.

But my sister filled the need
and tucked me in *her* arms to feed.
She wouldn't leave me on my own,
with mother tired to the bone.

Eventually, I'd close my eyes
and silence fretful baby cries.
I didn't know what I lacked then.
I couldn't see what should have been.

My sister, only just a teen,
filled the gap, the in-between.
She loved, and loving made a nest.
She loved, and loving gave me rest.

VII

Shepherd of
a Wayward Sheep

Any Day Now

I portray myself as a negative person.
Don't believe it for a moment.
In hardship, I pocket a living ember of hope,
with the capacity to eradicate all gloomy inclinations.
Any day now, a bird will lift its tiny head and sing.
I'll wash windows and discover jonquils bloomed
    overnight.
I'll smile, because God holds the threads, not me.
Any day now, He'll throw a handful of joy in
    His recipe
and pour it in my direction.

On My Own

To walk the distance of the day,
and toss the sleepless hours away.
To finally sleep in shallow dreams,
broken by the sun's first beams.
Life's a see-through curtain,
but what is seen there isn't certain.
It all depends on where you stand
a heart that *lives*,
wishes no end.
So I . . .
blossom in the presence of
a reason
and desire
to love.

When a Man Cries

What defines important conversation?
I propose: sincere connection
with those who give consideration.
Time taken.
Time shared.
Joy spoken.
Grievance aired.
But often those that can't express
feel much more deeply than the rest.
Something happens
when a hard man cries,
the tears escaping from his eyes.
A love that lingers far beyond,
A cherished memory, cherished bond.

The Becoming

Obedience.
Each being, being of its kind.
God said in the beginning
that this was good,
allowing
fulfillment of allotted gifts,
dreams
for myself and others.

I let go, and do not clutch
ancient grief or bitterness.
When mist in clouds
yearns for release,
it falls
as rain,
to touch the earth
where it belongs.

Where Flesh is Weak

I sometimes long to be alone,
friends tucked safely far away.
A place where I'd remain unknown,
with loneliness, no part to play.

Birds outside my window seat
calm anxious mind to quiet rest.
Their melody is free and sweet.
I envy them their feathered nest.

I am better for this space,
free of noise and endless chatter,
just my own to change the pace,
and only I can mend the matter.

Until . . .
When did it start,
this slow decay?
I thought it small
but it grew unabated.
Good nutrition?
Exercise?
Their walls are wearing down.
I carefully craft a disguise
and won't be seen without it.
But I am flesh *and* spirit,
a spirit that improves with age.
It partners now with wisdom
and abandons youthful confidence.

I Follow the Lamb

Little lamb, little lamb, show me the way.
I search for a child asleep on the hay.
I followed the shepherds; I followed a star.
Do you know, little lamb, is it yet far?
I heard for a moment, a heavenly throng,
and followed the voices of sweet angel song.

Little lamb, lead me to life's journey's end,
to the one they call Jesus, the one I call friend.
Oh, let me adore Him, and promise him love.
Oh, let me adore Him, this child from above.
Little lamb, dearest lamb, show me the way,
and gently I'll kneel by His bed of fresh hay.

In the hush of the darkness, I hear a faint cry.
I turn and I run toward a glow in the sky.
Just there, in a stable, so softly I tread.
Just there, in a manger, I touch His sweet head.
Joy to the Mother who gave the child birth!
Joy to mankind and peace be on earth!

The Pilgrim Road

Pilgrim, take your place.
Set the pace, run the race.
On your mark, get set, go!
Forward, backward,
ebb and flow
alongside the tides of life.

Short step first, then long stride
sail on wings of silver tide.
Stumble. Fall. Refuse to rise.
Lift your heart, lift your eyes.
See the journey to its end.
Home.
Home is 'round
just one more bend.

Even the Stones

I walk among the daffodils
inhaling boundless mystery,
creation dancing in the light
of innocence and destiny.

Instinct summons, they obey.
Leave behind cold winter's berth.
Arise, embrace the softened air,
bring grace and beauty to the earth.

Were you there on Calvary's hill?
Tender blossoms, tender hope
among the cruel and dark array,
of soldiers braced on grassy slope.

I wonder, did He smile to see
your dainty petals, graceful leaves,
as He stood, both trapped and free
among the men accused as thieves?

Naught destroys such Holy Life,
not cross nor whip nor crown of thorn,
or nails or spears or laughing scorn.

He rests awhile then lifts His head
as earthly life approaches end.
Somewhere in my heart I know,
the flowers bowed
and called Him friend.

Word Search

God made poets,
yes He did.
Always searching
for the perfect word,
well-placed, expressive.
Not to be mistreated.
We search tirelessly
for the essence
of soul's definition.
To see and identify the pain,
and Loveliness
in the midst of Struggle.
Stretching beyond obvious,
to read, as if blind,
the confines
of the heart.
God made poets,
yes He did.
And I may be one of them.

U Halo Tega (The Great Mystery)

I am messenger,
nature's clarion,
robed in scarlet.
Freedom's warrior.
Above the earth
yet of the earth.

I am word
to those who listen.
I am word
to hearts that open.
Word unspoken,
spirit heard.

I am gentle,
fierce, protective.
I am promise,
hope, surrender
I am parent,
brother, sister.
I am wind
and rainy weather.
I am cold
and heat together.
Music, dancing
beauty blending.

I am End,
and New Beginning.
I am Joy

that's never-ending.
I am Love
in each endeavor.
I am Light and Truth
FOREVER.

Acknowledgments

To Shatter Glass was edited by Mitchell Bogatz, Managing Editor of Mitchell Bogatz Editing Services, Goleta, California. In my search for an editor, I was instinctively drawn to Mr. Bogatz's website and was met with generosity, patience, and sensitivity that "kept me in the game." He is a teller of truth but never discouraging, and an unrelenting searcher for beauty and clarity. I was not permitted to fall short of our mutual goal: that the material be real and honest, and would help us to know ourselves. Mr. Bogatz, author, screenwriter, editor and teacher, can be contacted by email at mitchell@mitchellbogatz.com.

About *Iron Pen*

"O that my words were written down!
O that they were inscribed in a book!
O that with an iron pen and with lead
they were engraved on a rock forever!"
—Job 19:23–24

Outcast and utterly alone, Job pours out his anguish
to his Maker. From the depths of his pain, he reveals
a trust in God's goodness that is stronger than his
despair, giving humanity some of the most beautiful
and poetic verses of all time. Paraclete's Iron Pen
imprint is inspired by this spirit of unvarnished honesty
and tenacious hope.

IRON
PEN

Who We Are

As the publishing arm of the Community of Jesus, Paraclete Press presents a full expression of Christian belief and practice—from Catholic to Evangelical, from Protestant to Orthodox, reflecting the ecumenical charism of the Community and its dedication to sacred music, the fine arts, and the written word. We publish books, recordings, sheet music, and video/DVDs that nourish the vibrant life of the church and its people.

What We Are Doing

BOOKS | PARACLETE PRESS BOOKS show the richness and depth of what it means to be Christian. While Benedictine spirituality is at the heart of who we are and all that we do, our books reflect the Christian experience across many cultures, time periods, and houses of worship.

We have many series, including *Paraclete Essentials*; *Raven* (fiction); *Iron Pen* (poetry); *Paraclete Giants*; for children and adults, *All God's Creatures*, books about animals and faith; and *San Damiano Books*, focusing on Franciscan spirituality. Others include *Voices from the Monastery* (men and women monastics writing about living a spiritual life today), *Active Prayer*, and new for young readers: *The Pope's Cat*. We also specialize in gift books for children on the occasions of Baptism and First Communion, as well as other important times in a child's life, and books that bring creativity and liveliness to any adult spiritual life.

The MOUNT TABOR BOOKS series focuses on the arts and literature as well as liturgical worship and spirituality; it was created in conjunction with the Mount Tabor Ecumenical Centre for Art and Spirituality in Barga, Italy.

MUSIC | PARACLETE PRESS DISTRIBUTES RECORDINGS of the internationally acclaimed choir *Gloriæ Dei Cantores*, the *Gloriæ Dei Cantores Schola*, and the other instrumental artists of the *Arts Empowering Life Foundation*.

PARACLETE PRESS IS THE EXCLUSIVE NORTH AMERICAN DISTRIBUTOR for the Gregorian chant recordings from St. Peter's Abbey in Solesmes, France. Paraclete also carries all of the Solesmes chant publications for Mass and the Divine Office, as well as their academic research publications.

In addition, PARACLETE PRESS SHEET MUSIC publishes the work of today's finest composers of sacred choral music, annually reviewing over 1,000 works and releasing between 40 and 60 works for both choir and organ.

VIDEO | Our video/DVDs offer spiritual help, healing, and biblical guidance for a broad range of life issues including grief and loss, marriage, forgiveness, facing death, understanding suicide, bullying, addictions, Alzheimer's, and Christian formation.

Learn more about us at our website:
www.paracletepress.com
or phone us toll-free at 1.800.451.5006

SCAN
TO
READ

You may also be interested in these...

Flying Yellow: New and Selected Poems

Suzanne Underwood Rhodes

ISBN 978-1-64060-402-5 | Trade paperback | $19

"*Flying Yellow* is salvific poetry at its most reverent, a crucial blessed antidote for our irreverent world." —*Sofia Starnes*

Wing Over Wing: Poems

Julie Cadwallader Staub

ISBN 978-1-64060-000-3 | Trade paperback | $19

"*Wing Over Wing* offers a way to live with meaning, grace and an ever-hopeful heart tuned to healing and discovery." —*Naomi Shihab Nye*

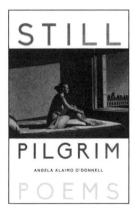

Still Pilgrim: Poems

Angela Alaimo O'Donnell

ISBN 978-1-61261-864-7 | Trade paperback | $19

"Angela Alaimo O'Donnell makes the daring move of including what has been considered undesirable subject matter for contemporary writers: the ordinary lived life of women, and the ardor and anguish of a religious life. *Still Pilgrim* is a remarkable achievement." —*Mary Gordon*

Available at bookstores Paraclete Press | 1-800-451-5006
www.paracletepress.com